SPORTS STARTERS

Kick it Soccer

Bobbie Kalman & John Crossingham

 Crabtree Publishing Company

www.crabtreebooks.com

SPORTS STARTERS

Created by Bobbie Kalman

Dedicated by Margaret Amy Salter
For Kian Reiach—the newest all-star athlete in the family

Editor-in-Chief
Bobbie Kalman

Writing team
Bobbie Kalman
John Crossingham

Substantive editor
Kelley MacAulay

Project editor
Michael Hodge

Editors
Molly Aloian
Rebecca Sjonger
Kathryn Smithyman

Photo research
Crystal Foxton

Design
Margaret Amy Salter

Production coordinator
Heather Fitzpatrick

Consultant
Jack Huckel, Director of Museum and Archives
National Soccer Hall of Fame, Oneonta NY

Illustrations *6761 2655*
Trevor Morgan: pages 6-7, 27

Photographs
© Rainer Holz/zefa/Corbis: page 19
Marc Crabtree: pages 8 (right), 9, 30
Icon SMI: Matthew Ashton: pages 26, 28; Scott Bales: pages 10-11, 13, 23, 29;
    Steven Bardens/Action Plus: pages 14, 17; John Gress: page 15; Andy Mead: page 22;
    Eric Swist: page 25; Bob Van Der Cruijsem/Pics United: page 24;
    Eric Verhoeven/Pics United: page 27
iStockphoto.com: Shelly Perry: page 31; Alberto Pomares: page 12; Patti Smith: page 5;
    Kirk Strickland: pages 3, 8 (left)
© Photosport.com: front cover, pages 4, 16, 20, 21
Other images by Adobe Image Library, Digital Stock, and Photodisc

Library and Archives Canada Cataloguing in Publication

Kalman, Bobbie, 1947-
    Kick it soccer / Bobbie Kalman & John Crossingham.

(Sports starters)
Includes index.
ISBN 978-0-7787-3138-2 (bound)
ISBN 978-0-7787-3170-2 (pbk.)

    1. Soccer--Juvenile literature. I. Crossingham, John, 1974-
II. Title. III. Series: Sports starters (St. Catharines, Ont.)

GV943.25.K34 2007   j796.334   C2007-900586-1

Library of Congress Cataloging-in-Publication Data

Kalman, Bobbie.
    Kick it soccer / Bobbie Kalman & John Crossingham.
       p. cm. -- (Sports starters)
    Includes index.
    ISBN-13: 978-0-7787-3138-2 (rlb)
    ISBN-10: 0-7787-3138-3 (rlb)
    ISBN-13: 978-0-7787-3170-2 (pb)
    ISBN-10: 0-7787-3170-7 (pb)
    1. Soccer--Juvenile literature. I. Crossingham, John, 1974- II. Title. III. Series.
    GV943.25.K35 2007
    796.334--dc22
                                                              2007002704

Crabtree Publishing Company

www.crabtreebooks.com   1-800-387-7650

Published in Canada
Crabtree Publishing
616 Welland Ave.
St. Catharines, ON
L2M 5V6

Published in the United States
Crabtree Publishing
PMB16A
350 Fifth Ave., Suite 3308
New York, NY 10118

Published in the United Kingdom
Crabtree Publishing
White Cross Mills
High Town, Lancaster
LA1 4XS

Published in Australia
Crabtree Publishing
386 Mt. Alexander Rd.
Ascot Vale (Melbourne)
VIC 3032

Contents

What is soccer?

Soccer is the most popular sport in the world. In soccer, two teams play against each other on a large field. There is a net at each end of the field. Each team tries to score **goals**, or points. A team scores goals by getting a ball into the other team's net.

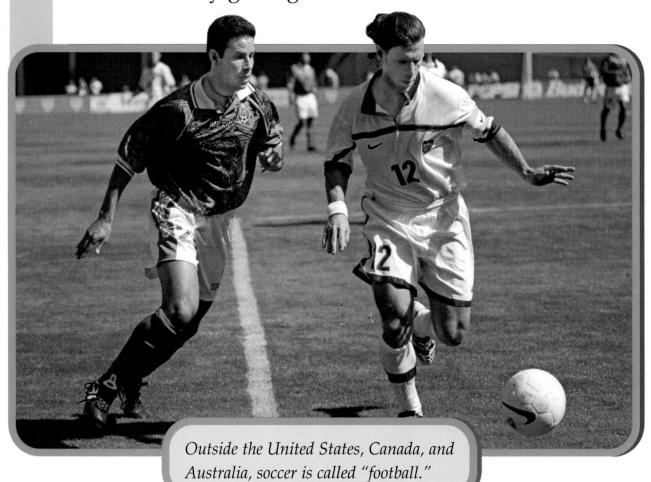

Outside the United States, Canada, and Australia, soccer is called "football."

Team players

Each soccer team has eleven **players**, or teammates. All the players are on the field at the same time. Most players can touch the ball with only their feet, legs, chests, or heads. The players move the ball mainly by kicking it.

Offense or defense

A soccer team is always playing **offense** or **defense**. A team plays offense when it has control of the ball and is trying to score. A team plays defense when it does not have control of the ball and is trying to stop its **opponents** from scoring. Opponents are players on the other team.

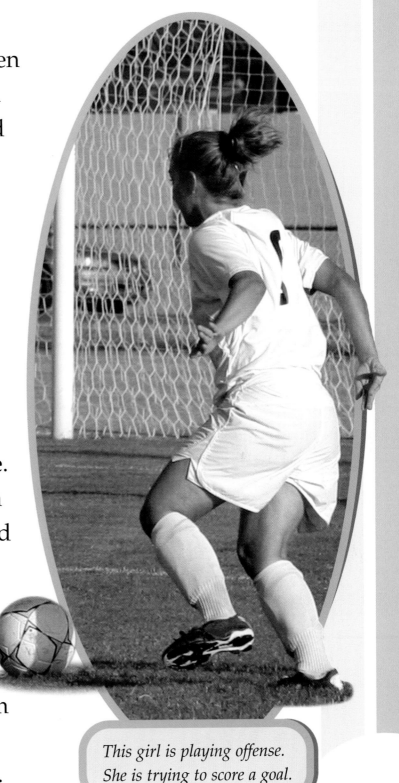

This girl is playing offense. She is trying to score a goal.

The big pitch

A soccer game is called a **match**. Two teams play a match on a field. The field is called a **pitch**. There are lines on the pitch. The **center line** divides the pitch in half. The **touch lines** mark the sides of the pitch. The **goal lines** mark the ends of the pitch.

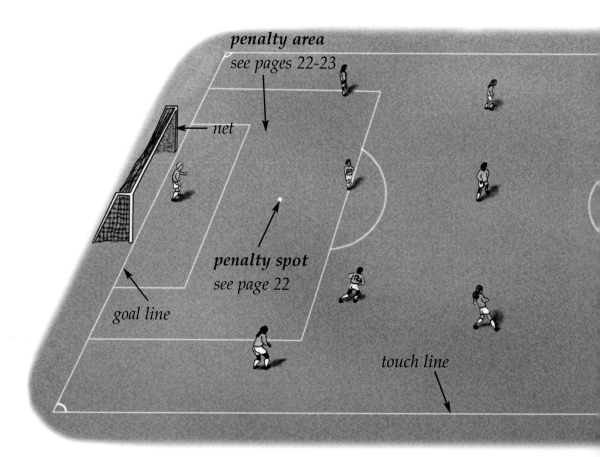

penalty area
see pages 22-23

net

penalty spot
see page 22

goal line

touch line

Positions, please

During a match, each soccer player does certain jobs to help his or her team win. The main jobs of the players depend on their **positions**. There are four positions in soccer. The positions are **goalkeeper**, **defender**, **midfielder**, and **forward**. Each team has one goalkeeper, four defenders, three midfielders, and three forwards.

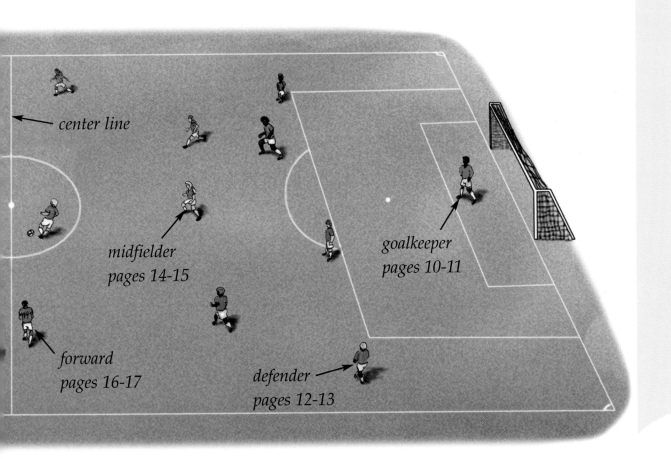

center line

midfielder
pages 14-15

goalkeeper
pages 10-11

forward
pages 16-17

defender
pages 12-13

Some main moves

Soccer players use many **moves**, or actions, to get the ball down the pitch toward the other team's net. Some of the main moves used in soccer are shown on these pages.

*To move the ball around the pitch, a player **kicks** the ball. The player kicks the ball by hitting it with her foot.*

*To move around the pitch with the ball, a player must **dribble** it. The player dribbles the ball by kicking it forward lightly as she runs.*

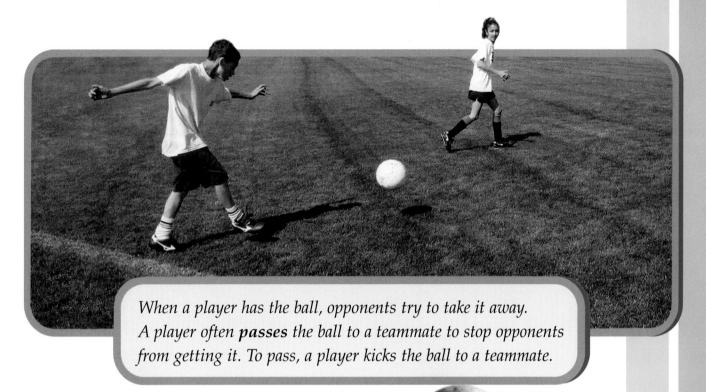

When a player has the ball, opponents try to take it away. A player often **passes** the ball to a teammate to stop opponents from getting it. To pass, a player kicks the ball to a teammate.

To get the ball away from an opponent, a player **tackles** the opponent. To tackle, a player moves very close to an opponent and kicks the ball away from her.

When a ball is in the air, a player can **head** it. To head the ball, the player hits it with her head. Heading the ball moves it back down onto the pitch or into the other team's net.

9

The keeper

The goalkeeper's job is to stop the ball from entering his team's net. Stopping the ball from entering the net is called a **save**. A goalkeeper is also called a **keeper**. The keeper is the only player who can touch the ball with his hands. *inside the box.* The keeper often uses his hands to make saves.

Super savers

Soccer nets are much taller and wider than keepers are! Keepers must be able to leap high into the air to make saves. They must also be able to move quickly in any direction to stop balls.

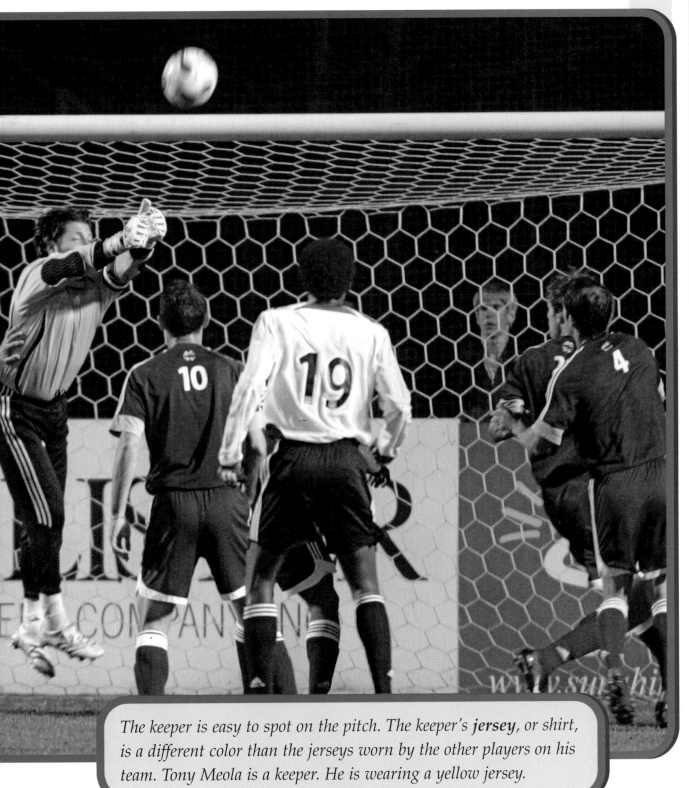

The keeper is easy to spot on the pitch. The keeper's **jersey**, or shirt, is a different color than the jerseys worn by the other players on his team. Tony Meola is a keeper. He is wearing a yellow jersey.

The defenders

Defenders try to protect their net from opponents. Defenders are also called **backs**. Each back stays close to a certain opponent. Staying close to an opponent is called **marking**. Backs mark opponents so that they can tackle those who run suddenly toward the net to score.

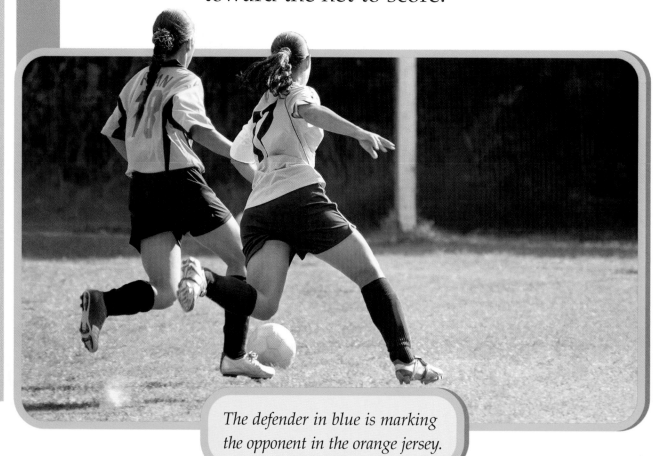

The defender in blue is marking the opponent in the orange jersey.

The player in blue is a back.
She has just tackled her opponent.

Tackles

Players must be careful when tackling.
There are rules about how tackles can be
made. Players must touch the ball before
they touch their opponents. Players cannot
push or trip opponents while tackling them.

The midfielders

Midfielders are good at playing defense. They try to get the ball by tackling their opponents. They also block passes. Midfielders are good at playing offense as well. They dribble the ball up the pitch and try to score goals.

This midfielder is dribbling the ball away from his net.

Thanks, I'll pass

Midfielders help their team keep **possession** of the ball. To keep possession means to stop opponents from taking the ball. Midfielders pass the ball to teammates to keep it from their opponents.

Clint Dempsey is an excellent midfielder. He is passing the ball to a teammate.

The forwards

Forwards have one main job. They try to score goals! All forwards must have great **shots**. A shot is a hard kick aimed at the net. A forward takes a shot in an attempt to score. A forward who has a great shot scores a lot of goals.

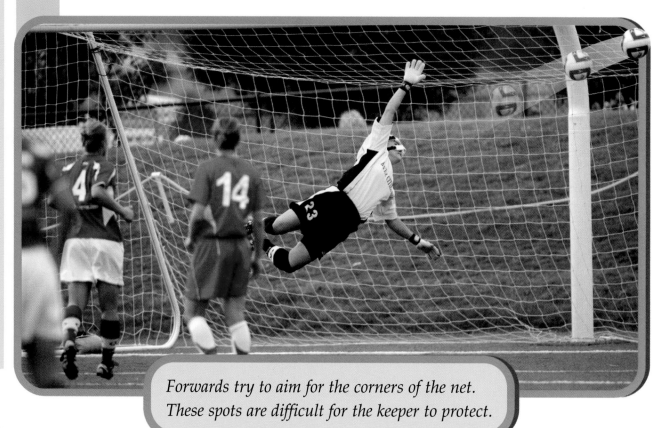

Forwards try to aim for the corners of the net. These spots are difficult for the keeper to protect.

Wayne Rooney is a forward. Here, he is taking a shot.

Great aim

Forwards practice their shots a lot. They practice aiming their shots at different parts of the net. During a game, forwards must take shots quickly. By practicing often, forwards learn to aim their shots so that the shots fly past keepers.

Keeping watch

There is a **referee** at every soccer match. A referee is the person who makes sure that all the players follow the rules. The referee watches the game from the pitch. He or she stops the game if a player **fouls** an opponent. A player fouls an opponent if he kicks the opponent instead of the ball.

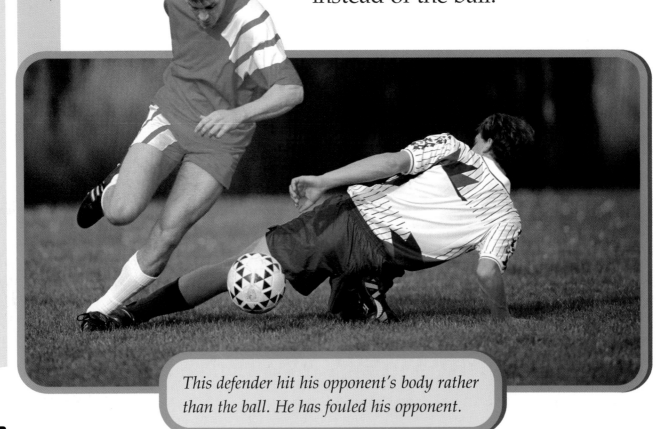

This defender hit his opponent's body rather than the ball. He has fouled his opponent.

Foul play

After a player fouls an opponent, the referee may show the player a **yellow card** or a **red card**. The yellow card warns the player that he or she must behave better. If a player hurts an opponent on purpose, the referee may show the player a red card. If a referee shows a player a red card, the player is out of the game!

If a referee shows a player a yellow card and the player still behaves badly, the referee will show the player a red card. The player must then leave the game!

Free kicks

When a player is fouled, the referee stops the game. A player from the team that was fouled gets to take a **free kick**. During a free kick, the ball is placed on the ground where the foul took place. The player taking the free kick then kicks the ball back into the game. The game starts again as soon as the player takes the free kick.

This player is placing the ball for a free kick.

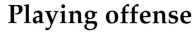

Playing offense

A free kick allows a team to take possession of the ball. The player that has the free kick can kick the ball to her teammates. They can then play offense. As a player takes a free kick, her teammates move forward to receive the ball. The team then works together to move the ball toward the opponent's net to score a goal.

This player is taking a free kick.

Penalty kicks

Sometimes players foul opponents inside the penalty area. When a player is fouled inside the penalty area, he or she takes a **penalty kick**. A penalty kick is a shot taken from the penalty spot. There is a penalty spot in front of each team's net. The keeper stays in the net to try to stop the shot. All the other players must wait outside the penalty area until the player kicks the ball.

It is difficult for even the best keepers to stop a penalty kick!

Shootout!

A match often ends in a **draw**. A draw happens when both teams have the same number of goals. When there is a draw, a **penalty shootout** takes place to decide which team wins the match. During a penalty shootout, each team takes five penalty kicks. The team that scores the most goals wins the match!

Leagues

There are soccer **leagues** all around the world. A league is a group of **clubs**, or teams. The clubs in a league play mainly against one another. Some clubs are over 100 years old! These pages show some famous leagues in North America and Europe.

FA Premier

FA Premier is an English league. It is home to many of the world's most popular clubs. Manchester United, Chelsea, Liverpool, and Arsenal are all FA Premier clubs. Cristiano Ronaldo, shown left, is a forward for Manchester United.

Ligue 1

Ligue 1 is a French league. Olympique Lyonnais, Olympique de Marseille, and Paris Saint-Germain are some of the clubs in Ligue 1. The league was created in 1932.

Major League Soccer

Major League Soccer is a North American league. It was started in 1996. Every year, the two top teams in this league play for the **MLS Cup**.

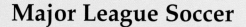

Primera

The Primera league in Spain includes clubs such as Real Madrid, FC Barcelona, Deportivo La Coruña, and Villarreal. Ronaldinho, shown right, is a midfielder who plays for FC Barcelona.

Going to Europe

The best soccer players in the world usually join clubs in Europe. The European clubs are part of the **Union of European Football Associations**, or **UEFA**. UEFA is the group that makes the rules for soccer in Europe. It also organizes **tournaments** for the clubs. A tournament is a series of games in which clubs play against each other for a prize.

The World Cup

The greatest tournament in soccer is the **World Cup**. The World Cup is held every four years. In the World Cup, players do not play for their regular teams. Instead, they play for their countries. A country's team is made up of players who were born in that country.

Fans from around the world go to World Cup games. People wave flags, paint their faces, and cheer for their countries.

Two tournaments

There are two World Cup tournaments—one for men and one for women. The women's tournament takes place one year after the men's tournament. In 2006, Germany **hosted** the Men's World Cup. In 2007, China will host the Women's World Cup.

Italy won the 2006 World Cup tournament in Germany.

Men's World Cup

Year	Winner	Host
2006	Italy	Germany
2002	Brazil	Korea/Japan
1998	France	France
1994	Brazil	USA

Women's World Cup

Year	Winner	Host
2003	Germany	USA
1999	USA	USA
1995	Norway	Sweden
1991	USA	China

World Cup trophy

Soccer superstars

There have been thousands of soccer stars over the years. Stars such as Pelé, Diego Maradona, David Beckham, and Mia Hamm have thrilled fans all over the world. Some of today's best players are shown on these pages.

Ronaldinho

Ronaldo de Assis Moreira is a great Brazilian midfielder. He is known as Ronaldinho. His dazzling dribbling and incredible passes have helped his team win many games.

Thierry Henry

Thierry Henry, shown right, is a French forward. He is known for making powerful shots. Very few players aim as well as Henry does! He is the leading goal scorer in the history of England's Arsenal club.

Gianluigi Buffon

Many people believe that Gianluigi Buffon is the best keeper in the world. His superb saves helped Italy win the World Cup in 2006.

Kristine Lilly

Kristine Lilly, shown left, is an American midfielder. She is the captain of the U.S. national team. Lilly has played more **international** matches than any other soccer player in history! She is also one of the top female scorers in history.

Steven Gerrard

When Steven Gerrard was a young boy, his favorite club was England's Liverpool. Today, he is a midfielder for Liverpool! Gerrard is one of the sport's best passers. He is also a great scorer.

Join a league!

Kids around the world play soccer. If you want to play, you can probably find a league nearby. Many schools have teams. Cities also have youth leagues that have teams for young people of all ages.

Playing team sports gives you the chance to make friends and have fun.

Camping out

Summer soccer camps are another fun way to learn to play soccer. Campers spend the day learning skills and playing matches against other kids. Ask a gym teacher or parent how to join a camp this summer!

Playing soccer is good exercise and a great way to stay healthy. Have fun!

Glossary

Note: Boldfaced words that are defined in the text may not appear in the glossary.

foul To break the rules of the game by making violent contact with an opponent

host To be the person, place, or organization that holds an event

international Describes a match that is played between teams from two different countries

MLS Cup The prize awarded to the top team in Major League Soccer

opponent A player who plays for the other team

penalty area The area of the pitch in front of the net where a foul leads to a penalty kick

penalty kick A kick taken from the penalty spot after a player is fouled in the penalty area

penalty spot The spot in front of the net from which a penalty kick is taken

position The job that a player has on his or her team

Index

Printed in the U.S.A.